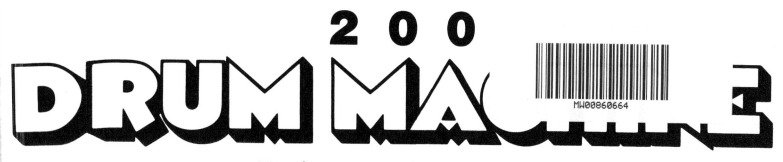

200
DRUM MACHINE
PATTERNS
By RENÉ-PIERRE BARDET

Contents

2 Preface
  Abbreviations
3 Grid Notation
4 Musical Notation
5 How To Use This Book
6 Useful Advice
7 Rhythm Patterns
  ROCK
12 FUNK
27 RHYTHM & BLUES
32 BALLAD
37 POP
42 REGGAE
47 DISCO
52 AFRO-CUBAN
57 BLUES
59 SWING
62 SHUFFLE
64 SAMBA
67 BOSSA NOVA
69 CHA-CHA
70 TWIST
72 SKA
73 ENDINGS
74 Original Patterns

ISBN 978-0-88188-632-0

HAL•LEONARD®
CORPORATION
7777 W. BLUEMOUND RD. P.O. BOX 13819 MILWAUKEE. WI 53213

Preface

You play guitar or keyboard, you make demo tapes, etc.

And, of course, in order to enrich your production, you decide to acquire a programmable drum machine.

After a few minutes of contemplation before the indispensable machine, you plunge into the user's manual for several hours. You understand the functions of each key. Then, feverishly, you plug it in and begin operating it.

The trickiest aspect here is rhythm programming. At this point, rock, the music you feel so strongly about, takes on all the allure of the "Wedding March." Reggae, which otherwise makes you come alive, becomes a dance for wooden ducks, and so on. You take one false step after another, you freeze, and begin to ask yourself just what you've gotten yourself into.

Do you find yourself asking this question? If you do, then this book is for you. Here, the programming problems you encounter are alleviated by 132 basic rhythm patterns and 68 corresponding breaks. Each of these patterns and breaks is presented in both musical notation and a "step time" grid.

If you've read your user's manual, you'll be able to program these patterns into your drum machine. This not only gives you immediate results with popular contemporary patterns, but also provides you with material that you can modify to your taste, and serves as a stepping-stone to programming patterns of your own.

NOTE: Since this book is designed to guide your first steps in programming your drum machine, the patterns have been kept as simple as possible. After mastering the material presented here, feel free to consult a more advanced programming guide in order to delve into such matters as triplets.

Abbreviations

Following are the abbreviations for the various elements that constitute the "drum set" found in drum machines.

AC: Accent	CH: Closed Hi-Hat
BD: Bass Drum	OH: Open Hi-Hat
SD: Snare Drum	CY: Cymbal
LT: Low Tom	RS: Rim Shot
MT: Medium Tom	CPS: Claps
HT: High Tom	CB: Cowbell

Grid Notation

The grid below is typical of those found in this book.

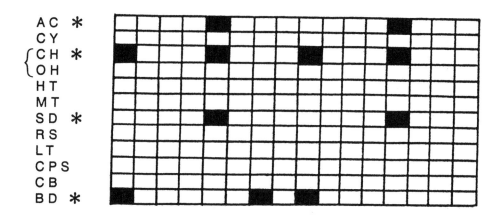

- Each grid represents a one-measure drum pattern.

- Each row of boxes in the grid represents one of the instruments in the drum set. An asterisk is placed next to each instrument that is used in that particular pattern. Thus, you can ignore the lines without asterisks.

- Each box in a row represents a unit of time. This unit is a sixteenth note (♪) or a sixteenth rest (𝄾), depending on whether the box is black (note) or white (rest).

Most patterns are in 4/4 time, as the example is. This means there are four quarter notes (♩) in a measure. The sixteenth-note unit used by drum machines allows each beat to be broken into four subdivisions. In simple mathematics:

- A quarter note is a quarter of a measure.

- A sixteenth note is a quarter of a quarter note, or a sixteenth of a measure.

A rhythm pattern in 4/4 time, such as that in the example, will therefore have 16 boxes in each row.

Because the sounds in a drum machine have a fixed duration (you can't play a "long note" on a snare drum; all you can do is hit it), the grids do not show the length of a drum sound. Rather, they show only the places where each drum is "hit."

Musical Notation

The literal translantion of the grid in the example into musical notation would be as follows:

literal
notation

Since this involves many short rests, however, common practice takes liberties with the notation, substituting longer note values for greater clarity:

common
notation

The following key shows how each element of the drum set is notated on the musical staff.

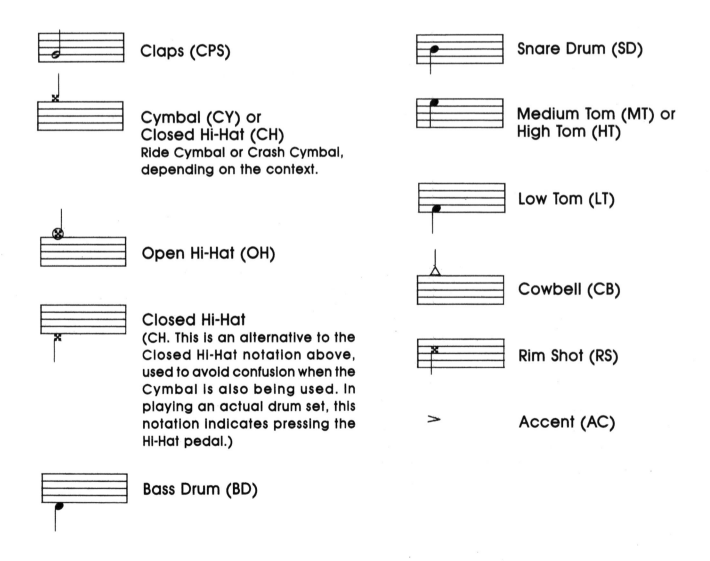

Claps (CPS)

Cymbal (CY) or
Closed Hi-Hat (CH)
Ride Cymbal or Crash Cymbal,
depending on the context.

Open Hi-Hat (OH)

Closed Hi-Hat
(CH. This is an alternative to the
Closed Hi-Hat notation above,
used to avoid confusion when the
Cymbal is also being used. In
playing an actual drum set, this
notation indicates pressing the
Hi-Hat pedal.)

Bass Drum (BD)

Snare Drum (SD)

Medium Tom (MT) or
High Tom (HT)

Low Tom (LT)

Cowbell (CB)

Rim Shot (RS)

>   Accent (AC)

How to Use this Book

1. Carefully read the user's manual for your drum machine in order to learn how to operate it in the WRITE (program rhythms) and the PLAY (listen to programmed rhythms) modes.

2. If you've chosen to program a pattern that is 16 units long (4/4 time; e.g., Rock or Pop), it is shown here by a grid that is 16 boxes across. If, on the other hand, you have chosen to program a 12-unit pattern (12/8 time, or less frequently, 3/4 time; e.g., Blues or Funk 15), it is shown here by a grid that is 12 boxes across (in 12/8 time, each box represents an eighth note rather than a sixteenth note). Select the appropriate pattern length on your drum machine.

3. Activate the WRITE mode.

   Using the example: Rock 1, Measure A

   a) Program AC (Accent):

AC ✳

   4 silences − 1 note − 7 silences − 1 note - 3 silences

   (4 + 1 + 7 + 1 + 3 = 16)

   b) Program CH (Closed High-Hat):

CH ✳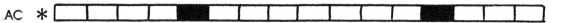

   1 note − 3 silences − 1 note − 3 silences − 1 note − 3 silences − 1 note − 3 silences

   (1 + 3 + 1 + 3 + 1 + 3 + 1+ 3 = 16)

   c) Program SD (Snare Drum):

SD ✳

   4 silences − 1 note − 7 silences − 1 note − 3 silences

   (4 + 1 + 7 + 1 + 3 = 16)

   d) Program BD (Bass Drum):

BD ✳

   1 note − 5 silences − 1 note − 1 silence − 1 note − 7 silences

   (1 + 5 + 1 + 1 + 1 + 7 = 16)

4. Switch to PLAY mode and listen to the rhythm.

5. Adjust the tempo to your taste.

Useful Advice

You have just programmed Rock 1 measure A; next you will program measure B, then the break. Programming of breaks, done exactly in the same manner as other rhythm programming, requires perhaps a little more attention because the number of percussion sounds used is more important.

You can then combine these three patterns as you wish:

Measure: A + B + A + B + Break

or A + A + Break + B + B + Break

or A + A + B + B + A + Break

etc.

The cymbal parts, which have been consistently indicated for Closed Hi-Hat (CH), you may wish to program for the Cymbal (sometimes called "Ride Cymbal"; CY). You may also wish to add Claps (CPS) or High Tom (HT) to underscore accents, and so on, keeping in mind, obviously, the capabilities of your machine.

This book is absolutely not a substitute for your imagination. It is designed to help you in putting basic rhythms into place, but it's up to you to personalize them. An infinite variety of rhythmic combinations lies at your disposal.

Rock 1

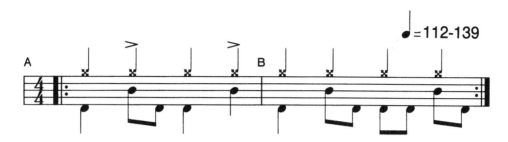

MEASURE A

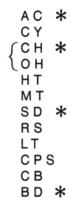
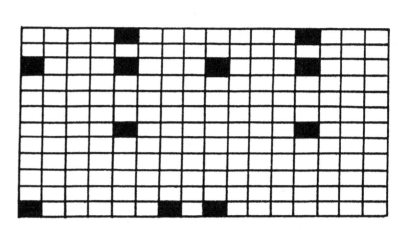

MEASURE B

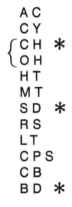
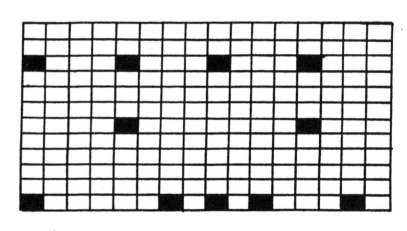

BREAK

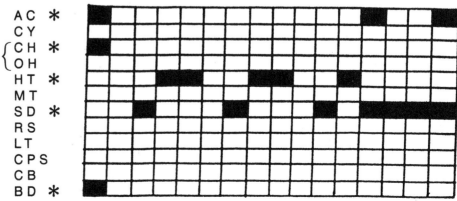

Rock 2

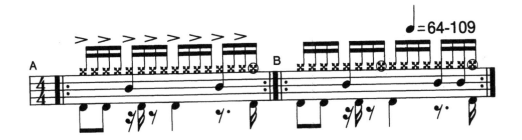

MEASURE A

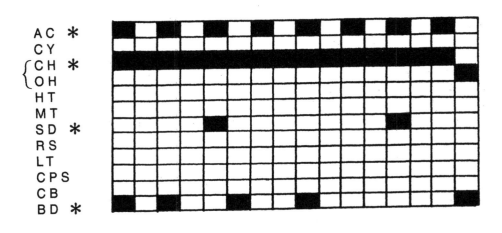

MEASURE B

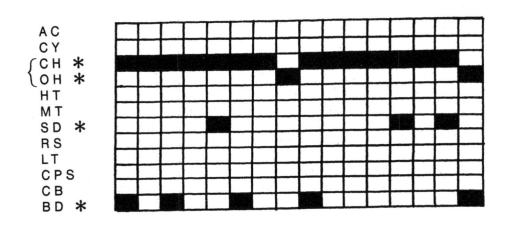

BREAK

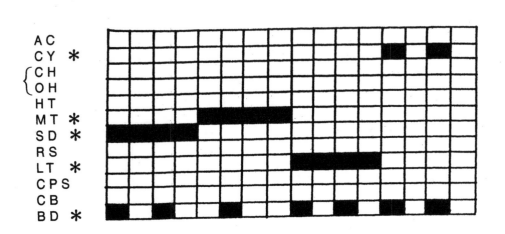

8

Rock 3

MEASURE A

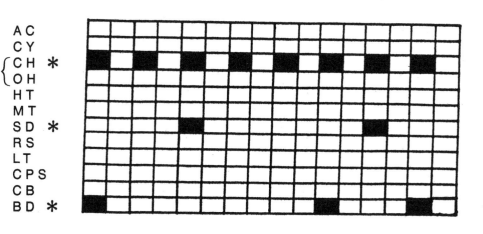

MEASURE B

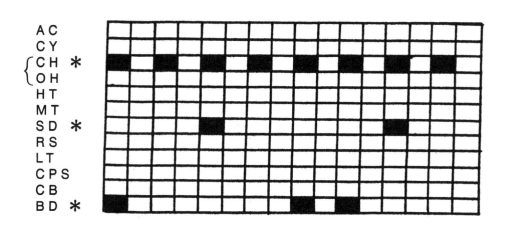

BREAK

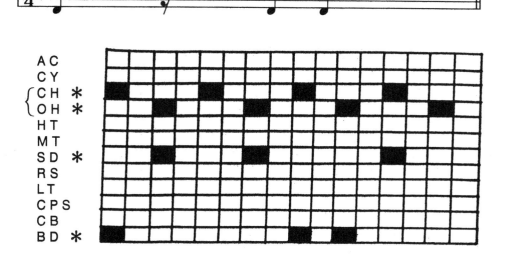

Rock 4

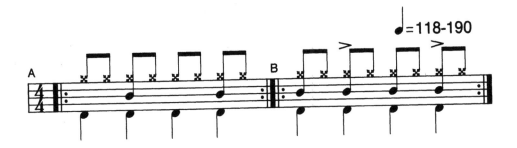

MEASURE A

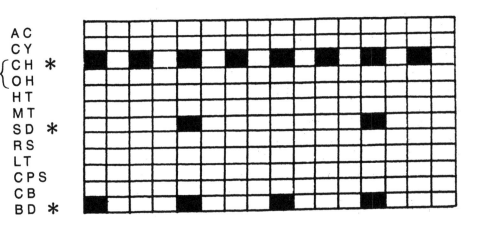

MEASURE B

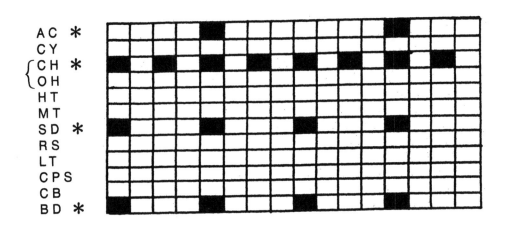

BREAK

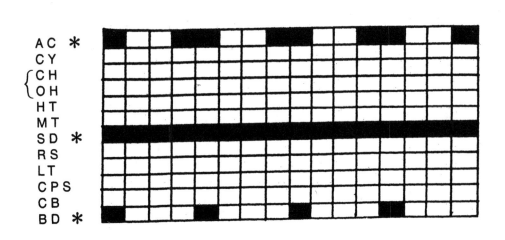

Rock 5

MEASURE A

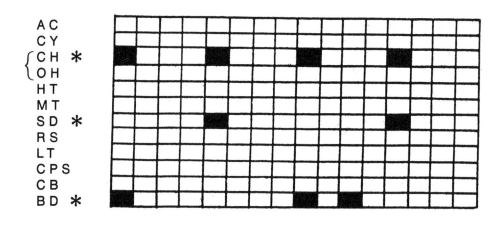

MEASURE B

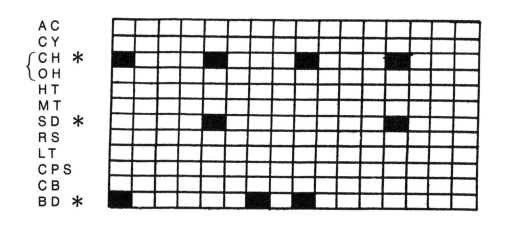

BREAK

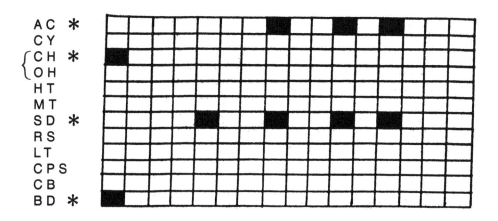

Funk 1

MEASURE A

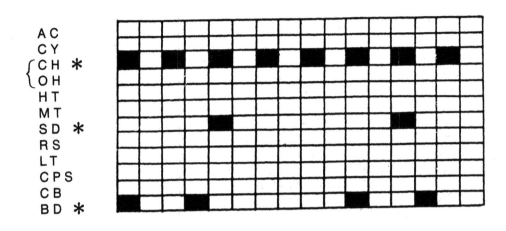

MEASURE B

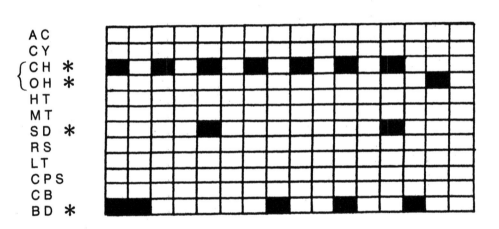

BREAK

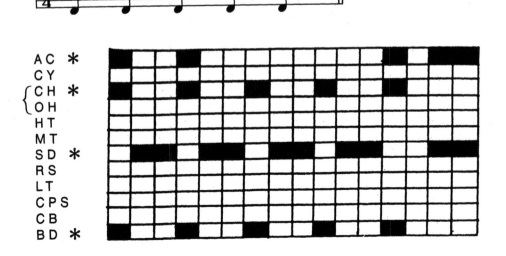

12

Funk 2

MEASURE A

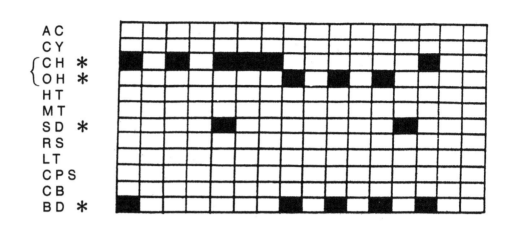

MEASURE B

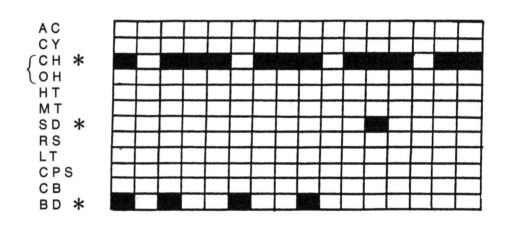

BREAK

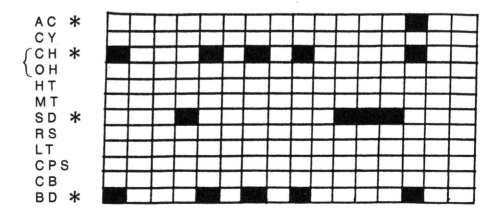

Funk 3

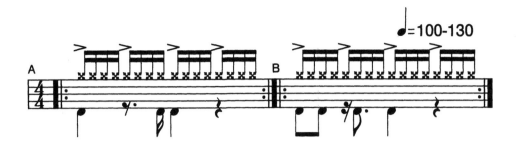

MEASURE A

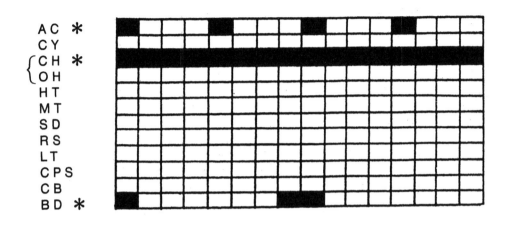

MEASURE B

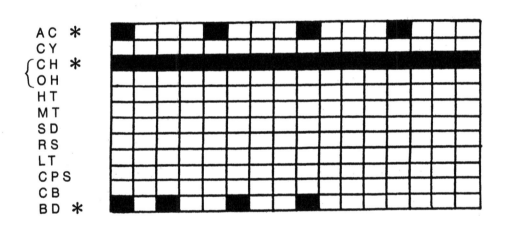

BREAK

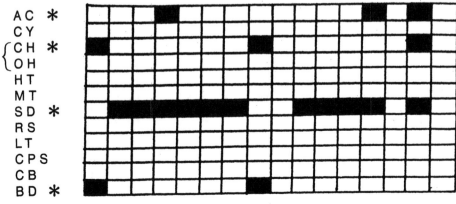

14

Funk 4

MEASURE A

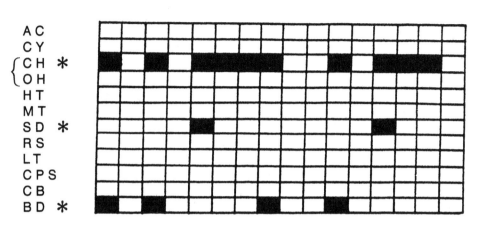

MEASURE B

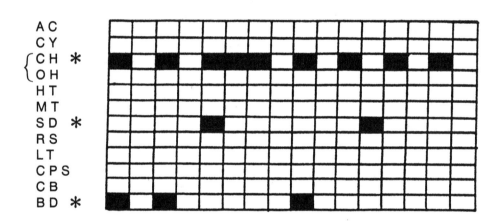

BREAK

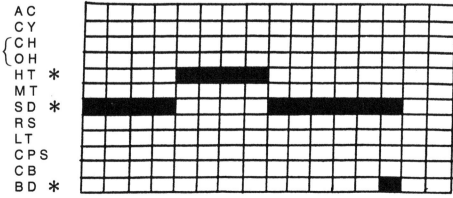

Funk 5

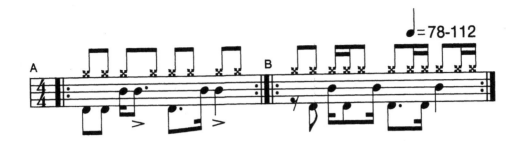

MEASURE A

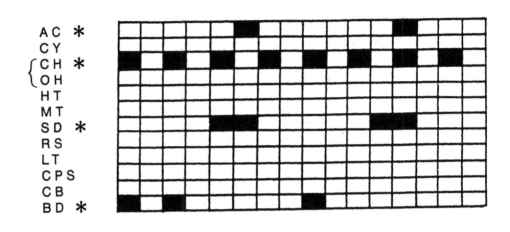

MEASURE B

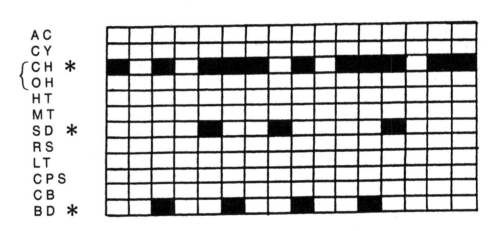

BREAK

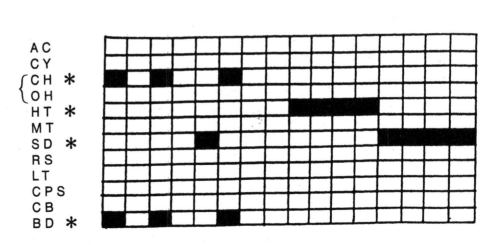

16

Funk 6

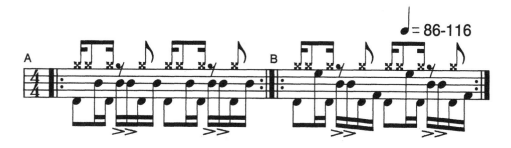

MEASURE A

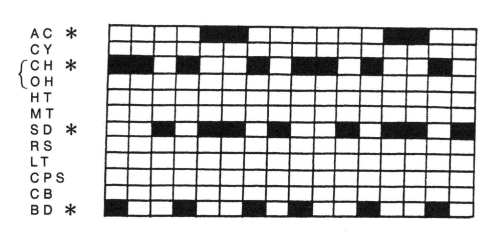

MEASURE B

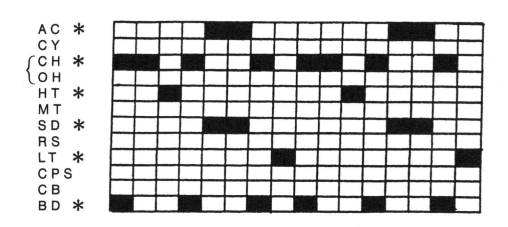

BREAK

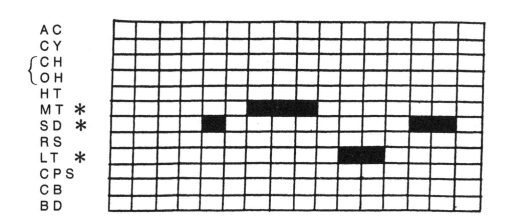

Funk 7

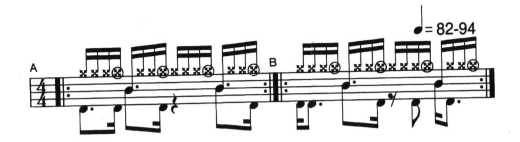

MEASURE A

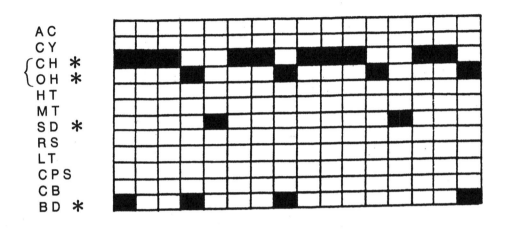

MEASURE B

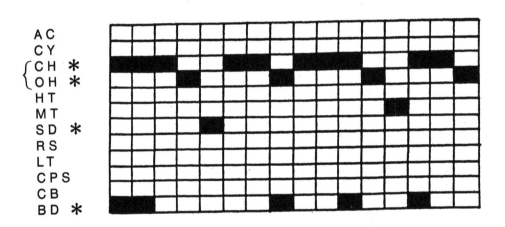

BREAK

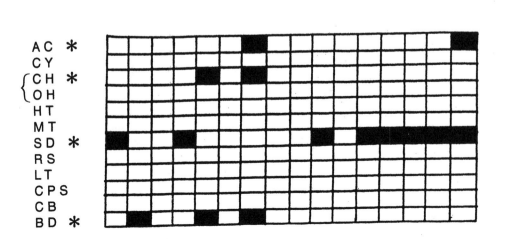

Funk 8

MEASURE A

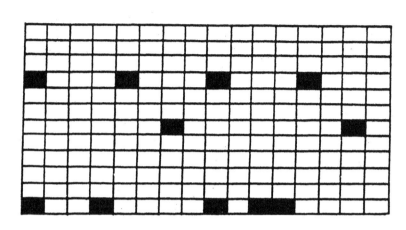

MEASURE B

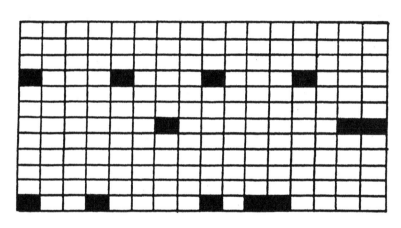

BREAK

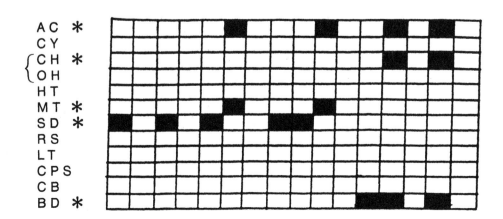

Funk 9

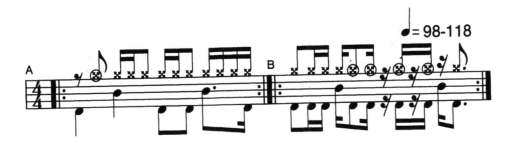

MEASURE A

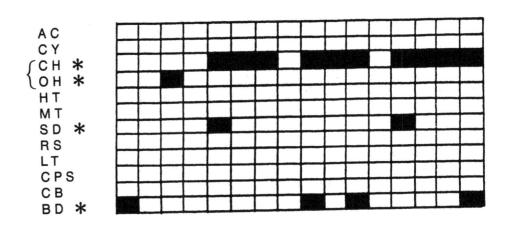

MEASURE B

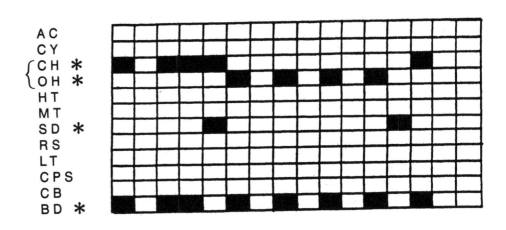

BREAK

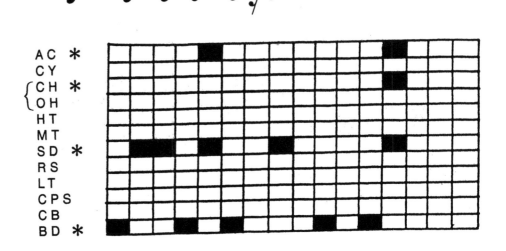

20

Funk 10

MEASURE A

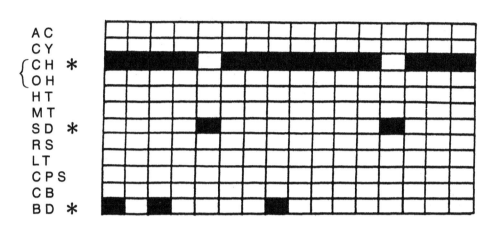

MEASURE B

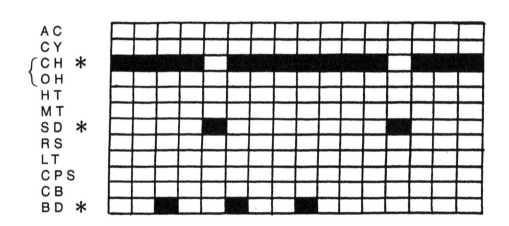

BREAK

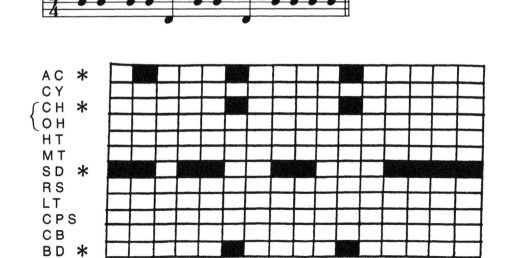

21

Funk 11

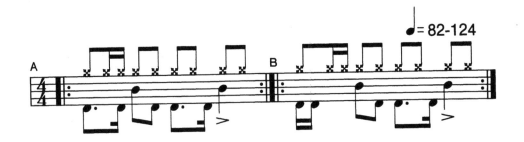

MEASURE A

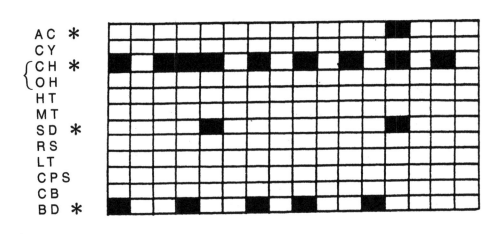

MEASURE B

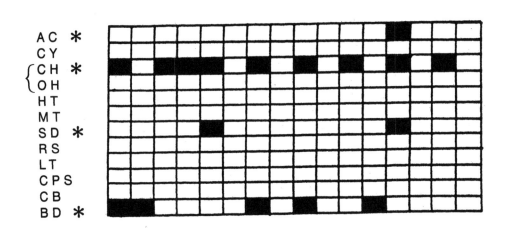

BREAK

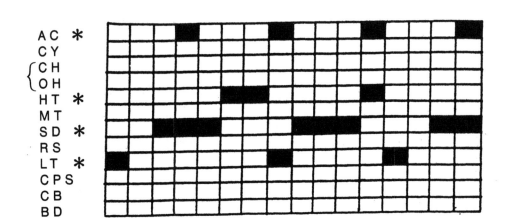

Funk 12

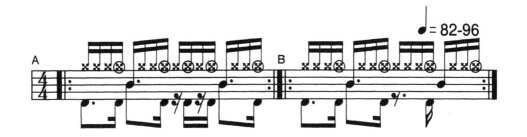

MEASURE A

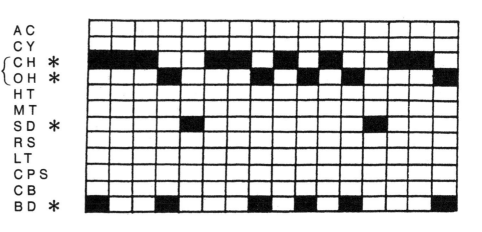

MEASURE B

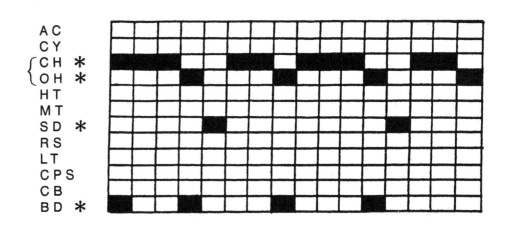

BREAK

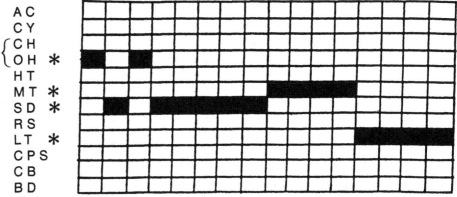

Funk 13

MEASURE A

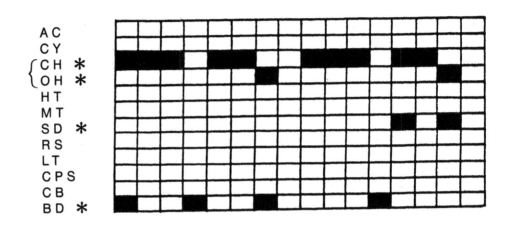

MEASURE B

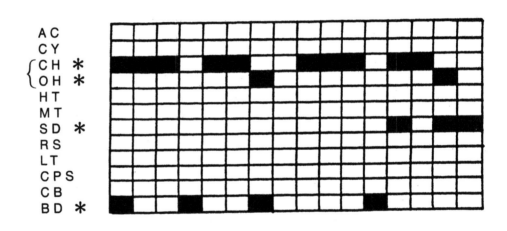

BREAK

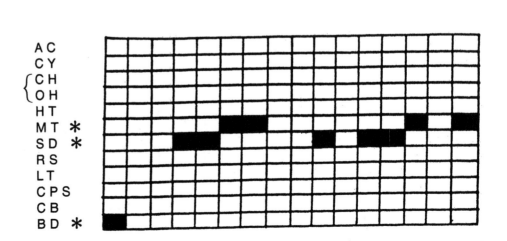

Funk 14

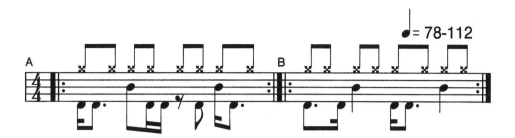

MEASURE A

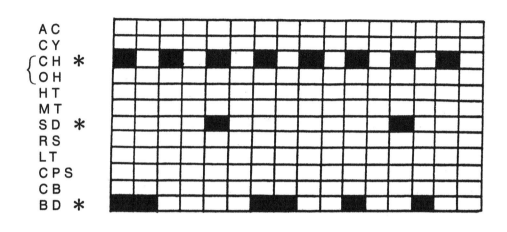

MEASURE B

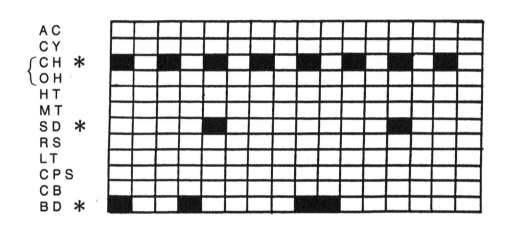

BREAK

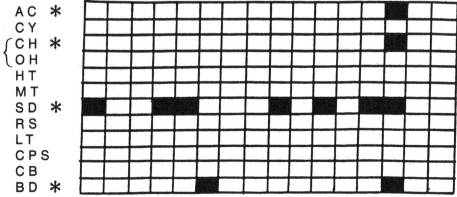

Funk 15

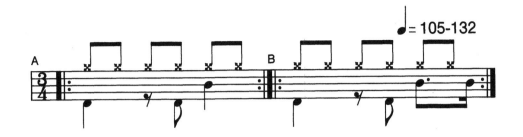

MEASURE A

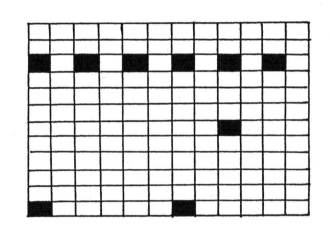

MEASURE B

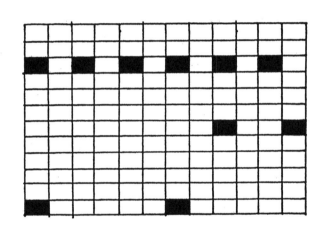

BREAK

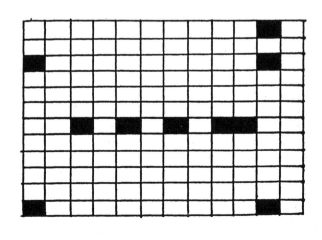

Rhythm & Blues 1

MEASURE A

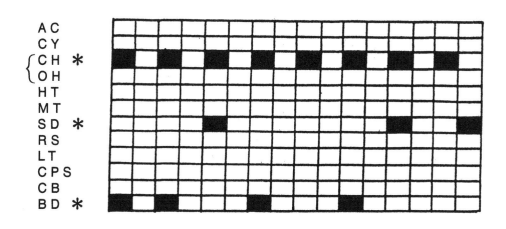

MEASURE B

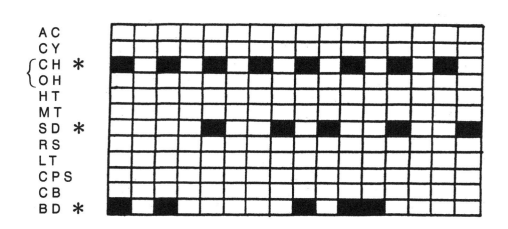

BREAK

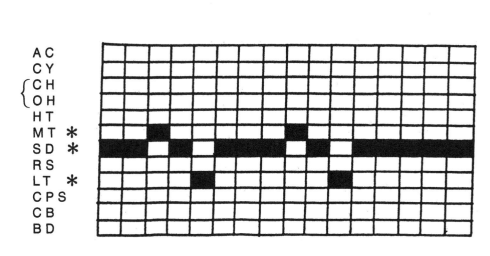

Rhythm & Blues 2

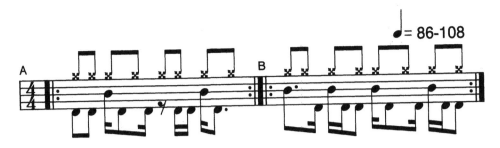

MEASURE A

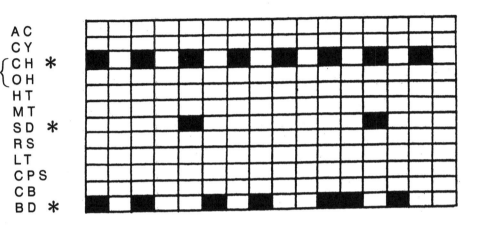

MEASURE B

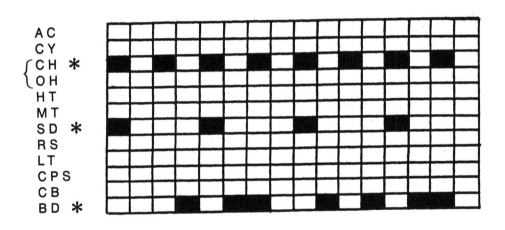

BREAK

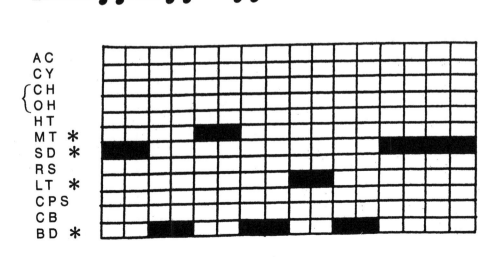

28

Rhythm & Blues 3

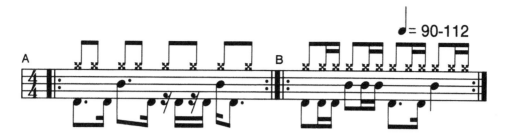

MEASURE A

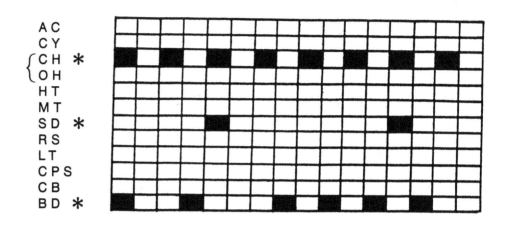

MEASURE B

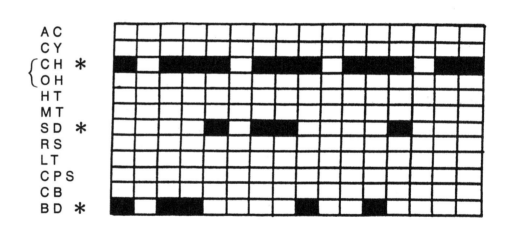

BREAK

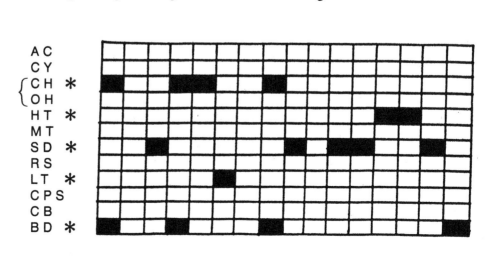

Rhythm & Blues 4

MEASURE A

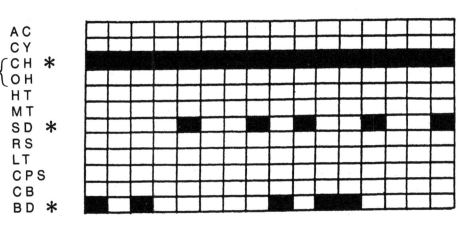

MEASURE B

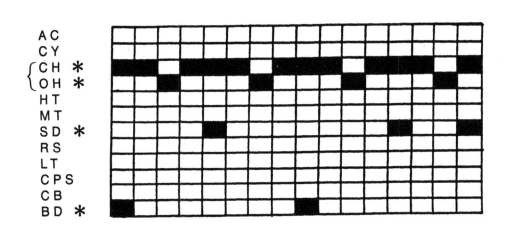

BREAK

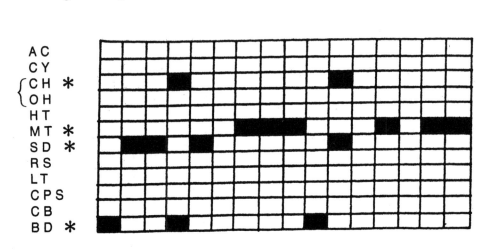

Rhythm & Blues 5

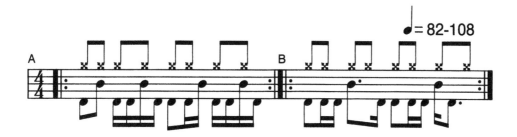

MEASURE A

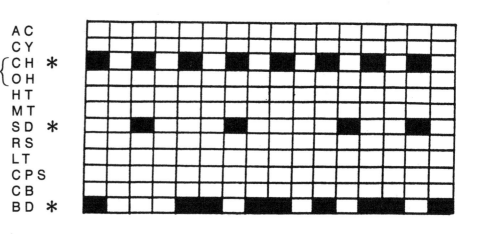

MEASURE B

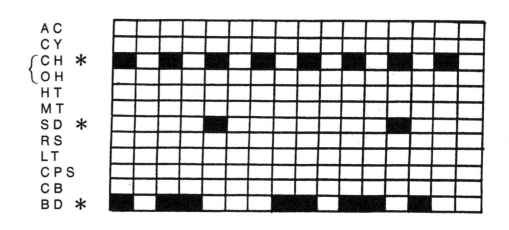

BREAK

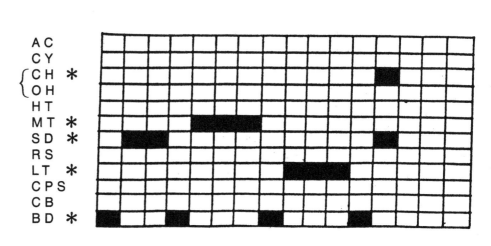

Ballad 1

MEASURE A

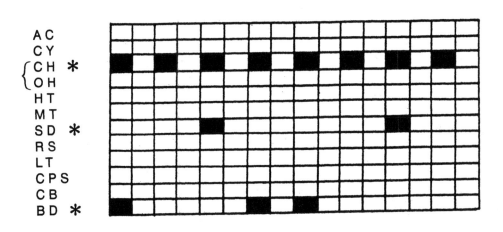

MEASURE B

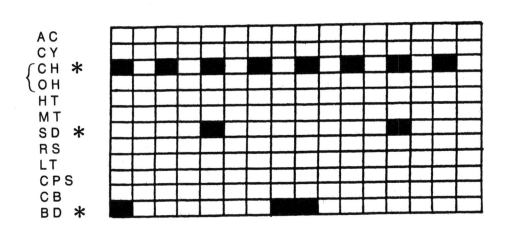

BREAK

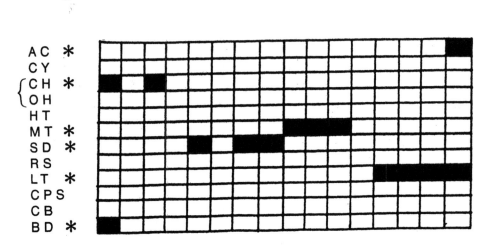

Ballad 2

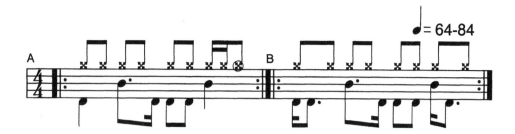

MEASURE A

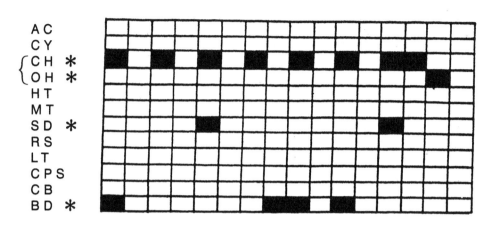

MEASURE B

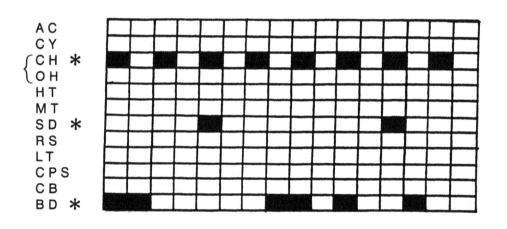

BREAK

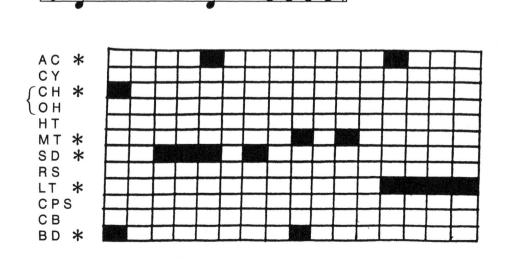

Ballad 3

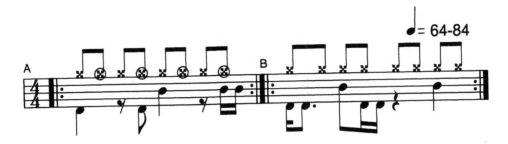

MEASURE A

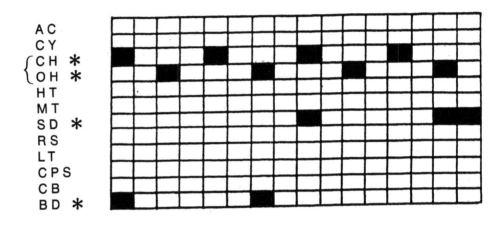

MEASURE B

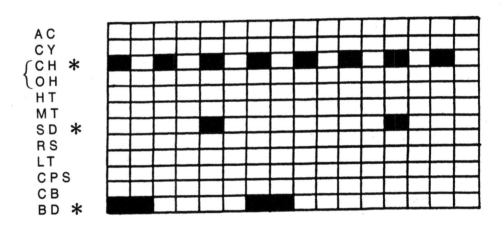

BREAK

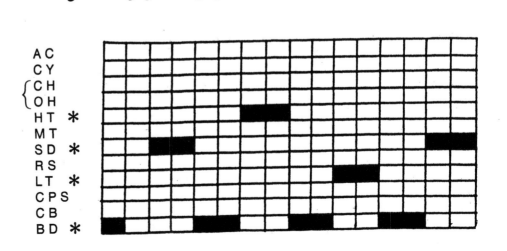

Ballad 4

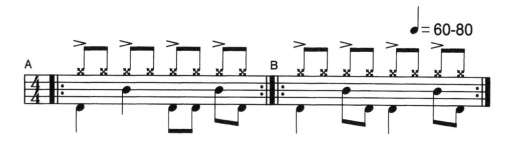

MEASURE A

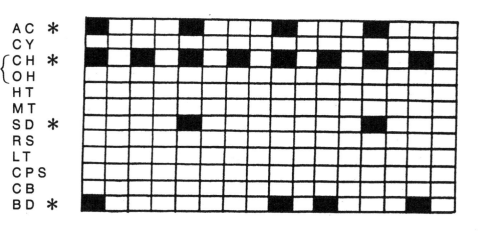

MEASURE B

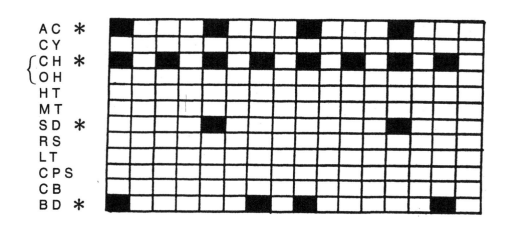

BREAK

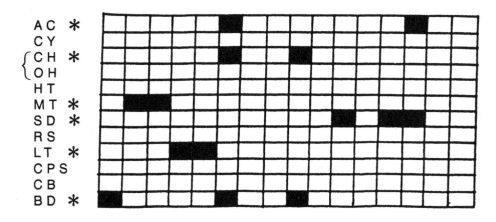

Ballad 5

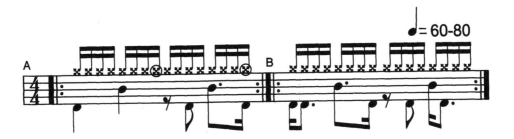

MEASURE A

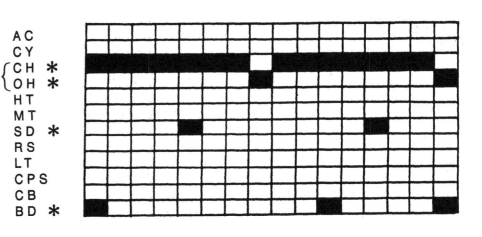

MEASURE B

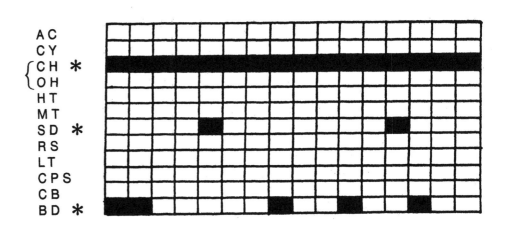

BREAK

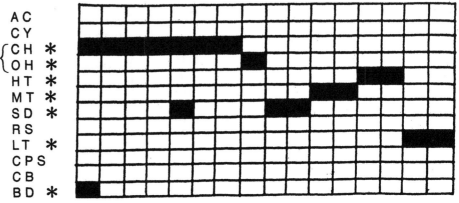

Pop 1

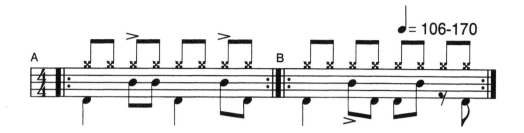

MEASURE A

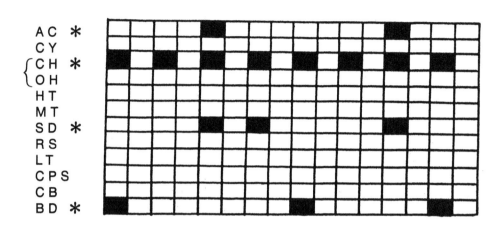

MEASURE B

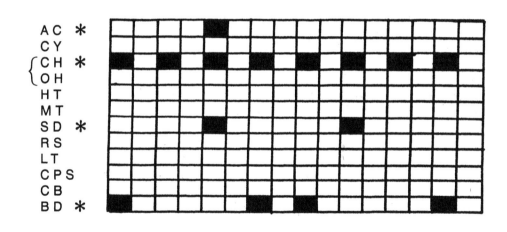

BREAK

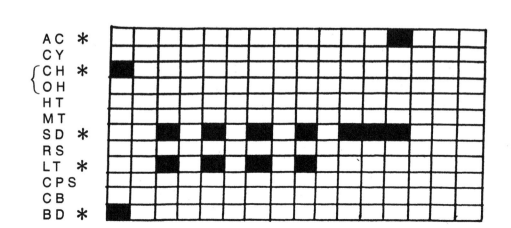

Pop 2

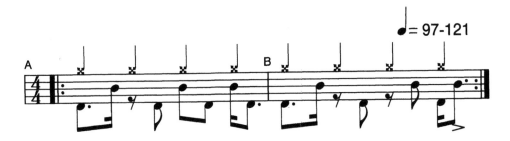

MEASURE A

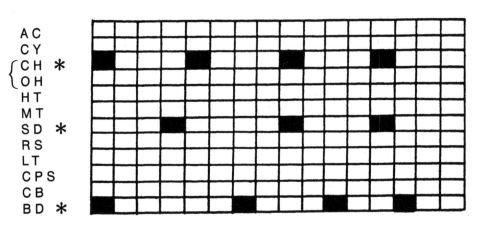

MEASURE B

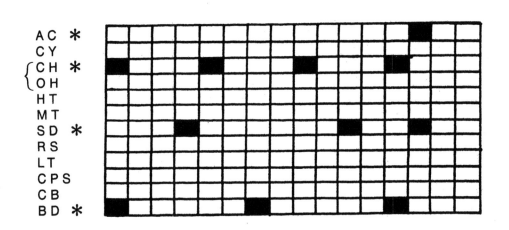

BREAK

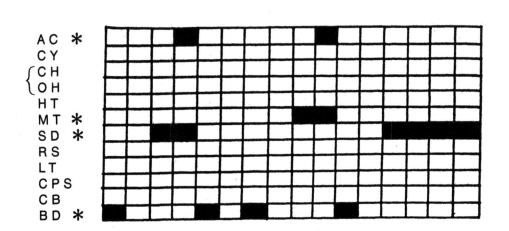

Pop 3

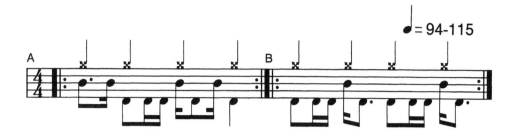

MEASURE A

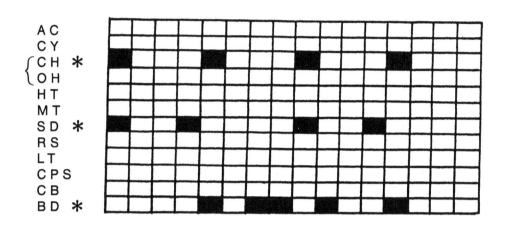

MEASURE B

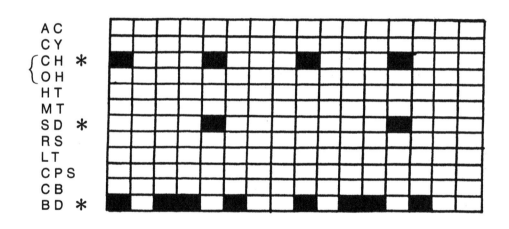

BREAK

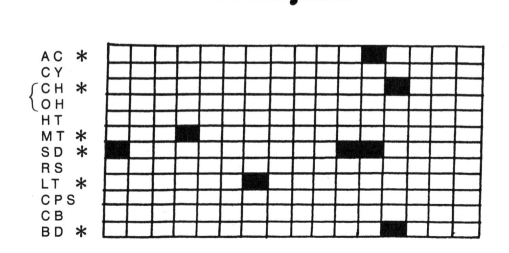

Pop 4

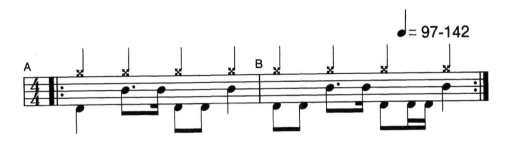

MEASURE A

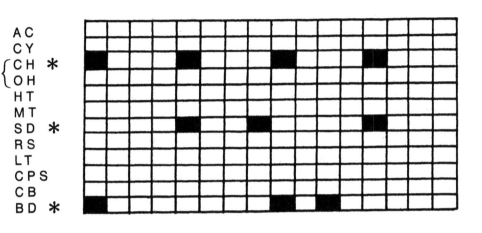

MEASURE B

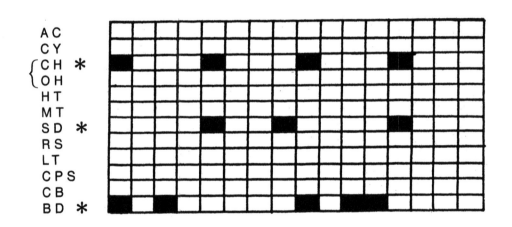

BREAK

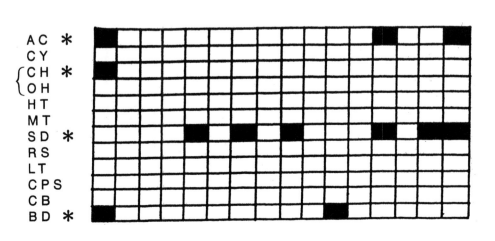

Pop 5

MEASURE A

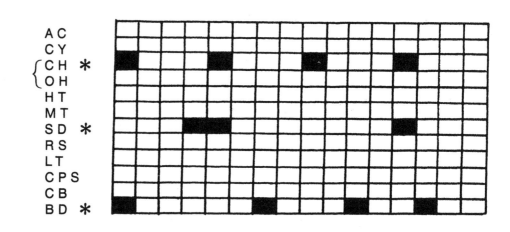

MEASURE B

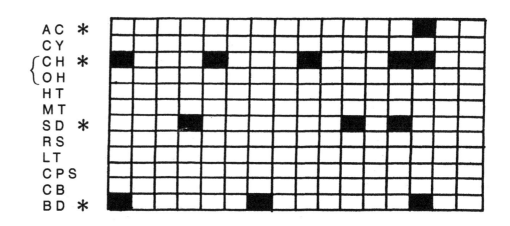

BREAK

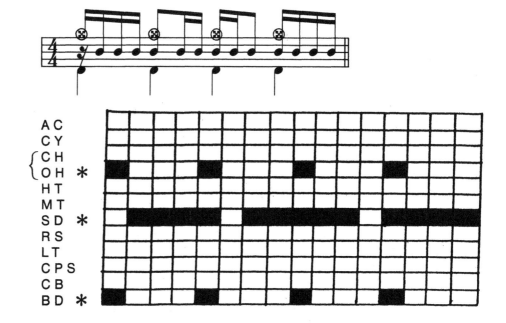

Reggae 1

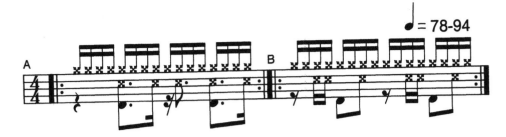

MEASURE A

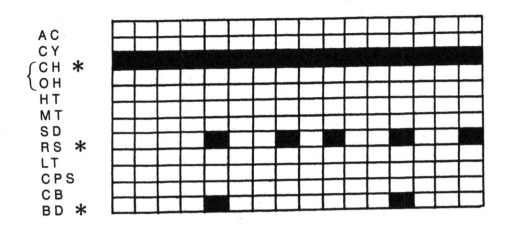

MEASURE B

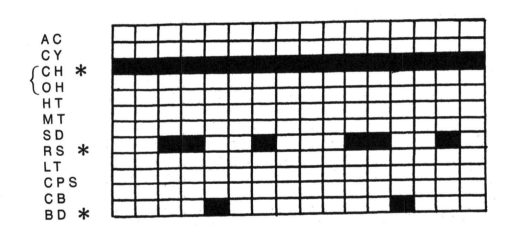

BREAK

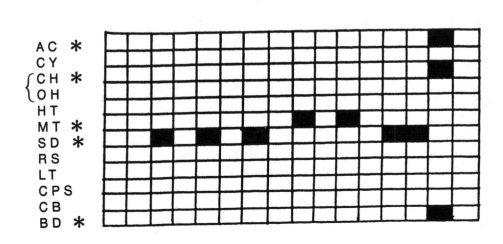

Reggae 2

♩ = 116-130

MEASURE A

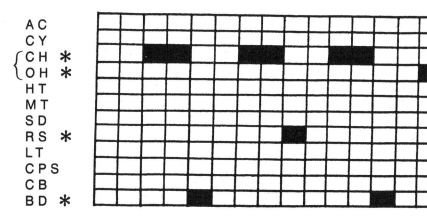

MEASURE B

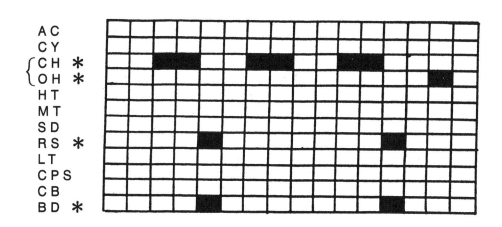

BREAK

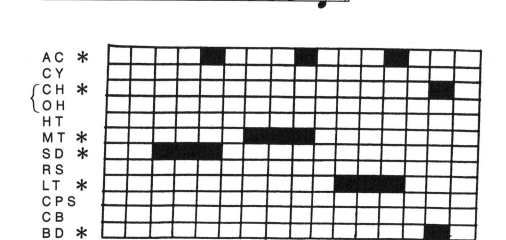

Reggae 3

MEASURE A

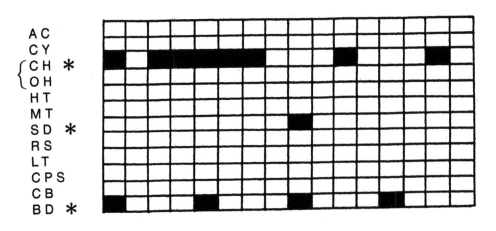

MEASURE B

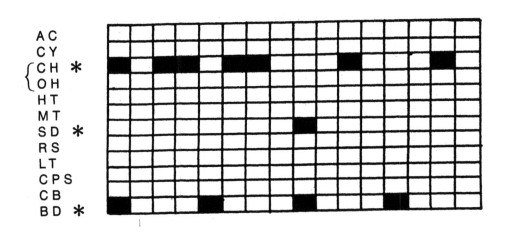

BREAK

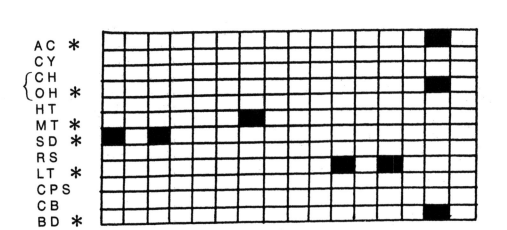

44

Reggae 4

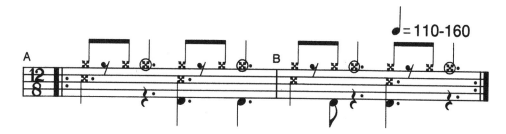

MEASURE A

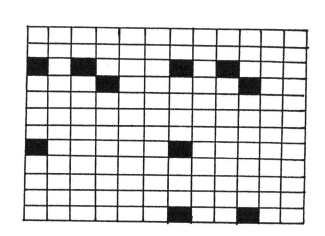

MEASURE B

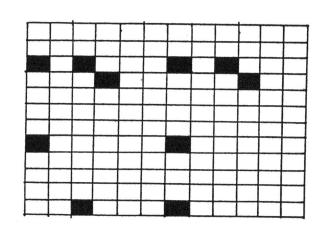

BREAK

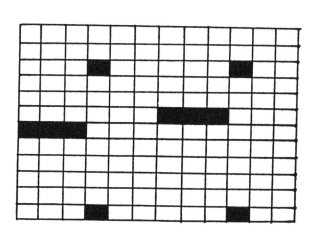

Reggae 5

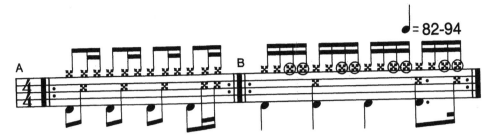

MEASURE A

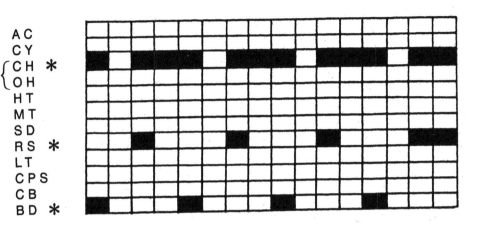

MEASURE B

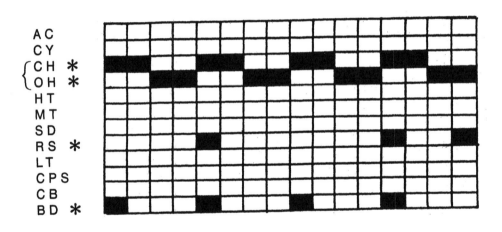

BREAK

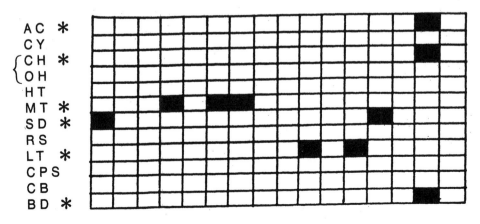

Disco 1

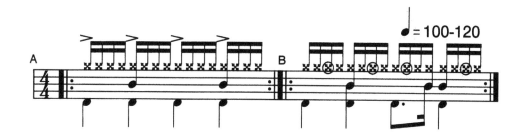

MEASURE A

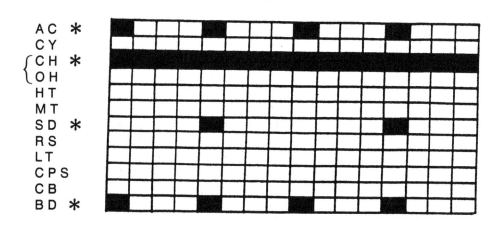

MEASURE B

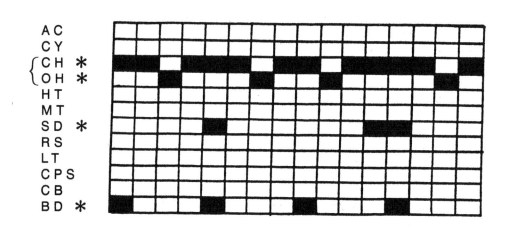

BREAK

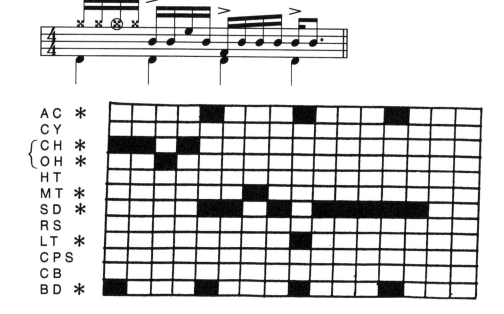

47

Disco 2

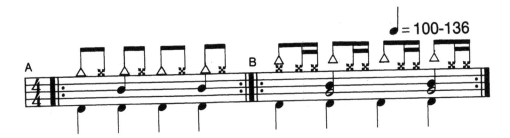

MEASURE A

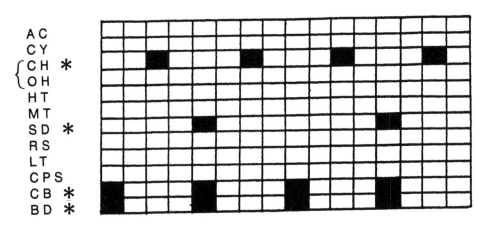

MEASURE B

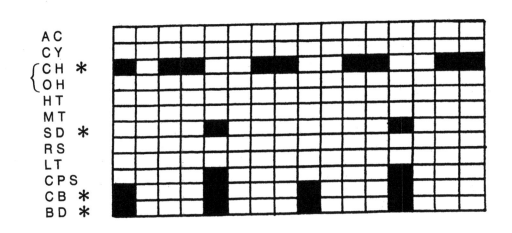

BREAK

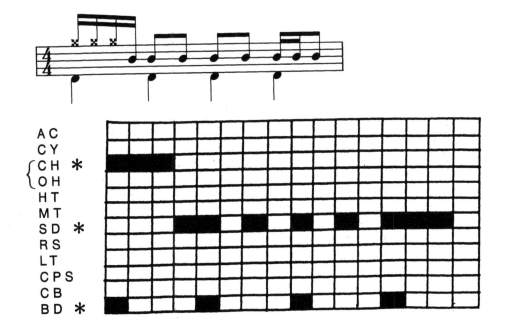

Disco 3

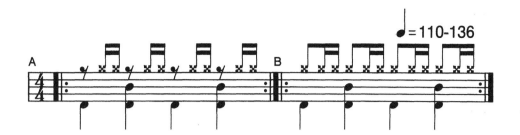

MEASURE A

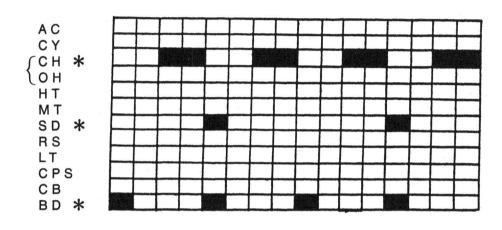

MEASURE B

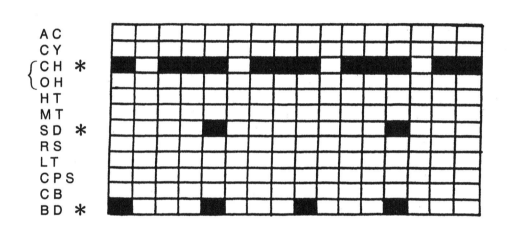

BREAK

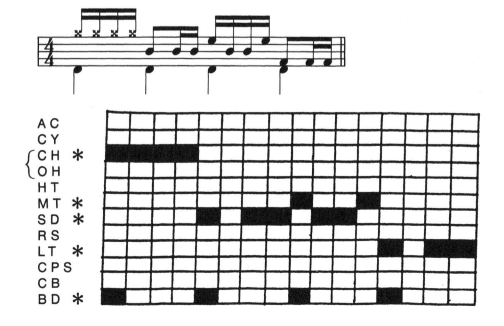

Disco 4

MEASURE A

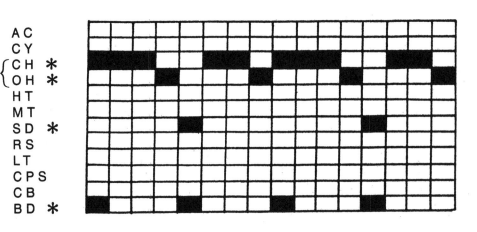

MEASURE B

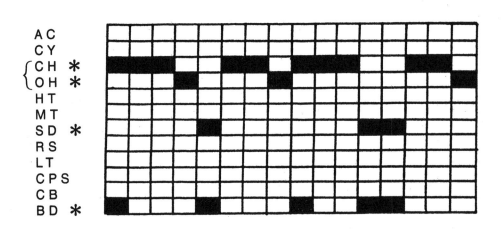

BREAK

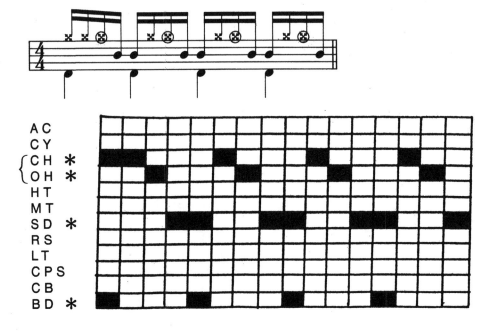

Disco 5

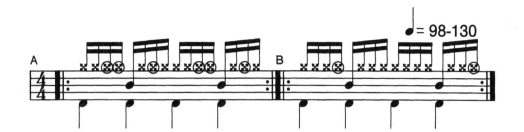

MEASURE A

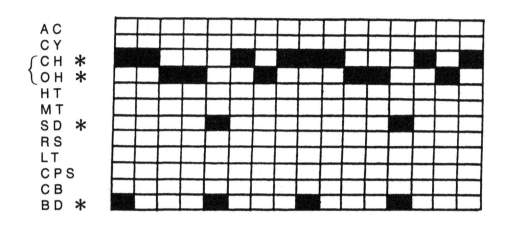

MEASURE B

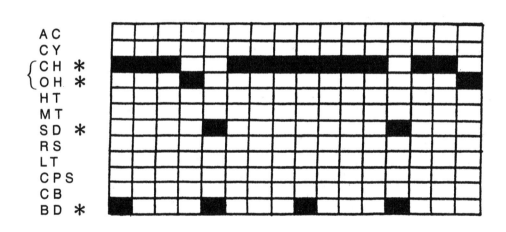

BREAK

Afro-Cuban 1

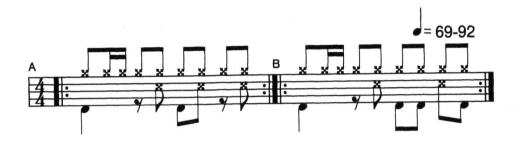

MEASURE A

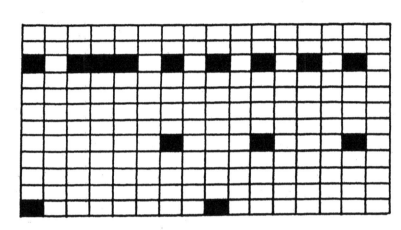

MEASURE B

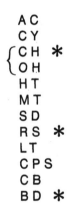

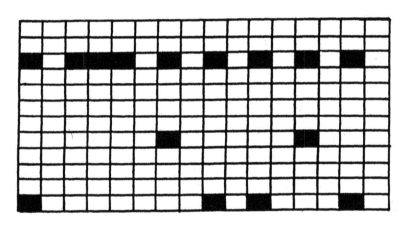

BREAK

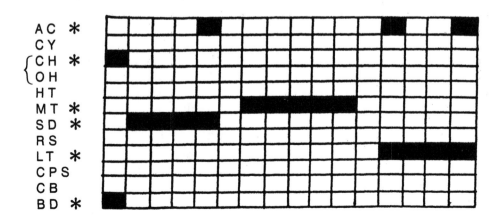

Afro-Cuban 2

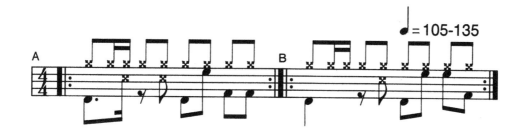

MEASURE A

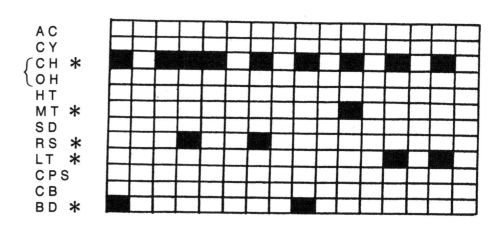

MEASURE B

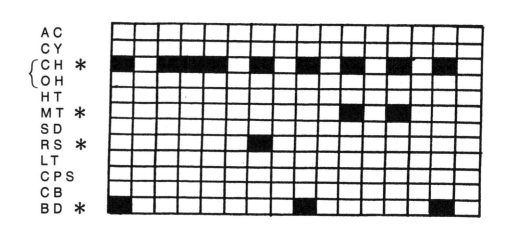

BREAK

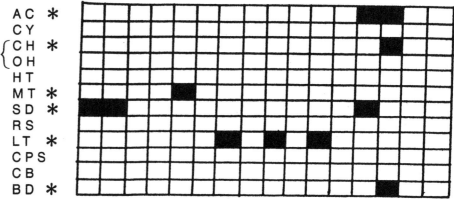

Afro-Cuban 3

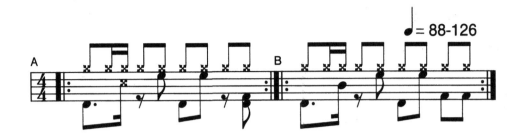

MEASURE A

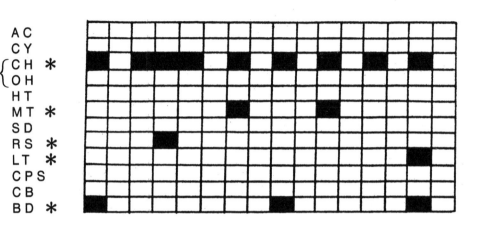

MEASURE B

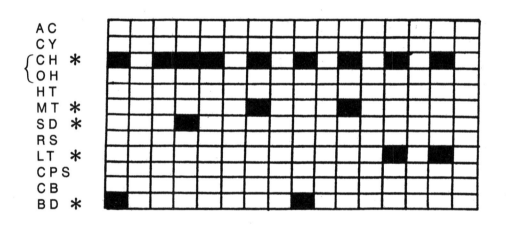

BREAK

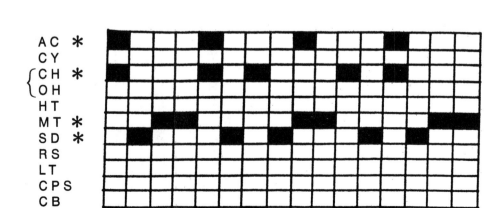

54

Afro-Cuban 4

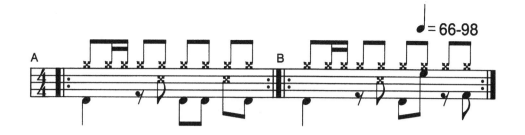

MEASURE A

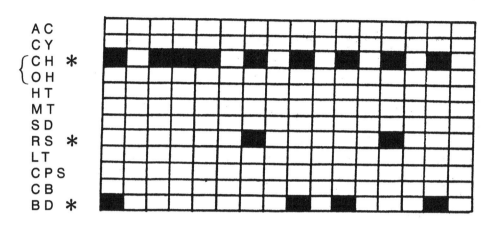

MEASURE B

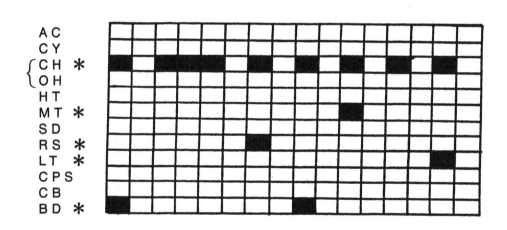

BREAK

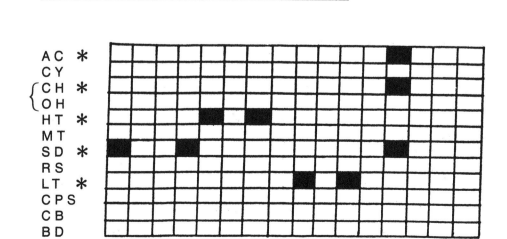

55

Afro-Cuban 5

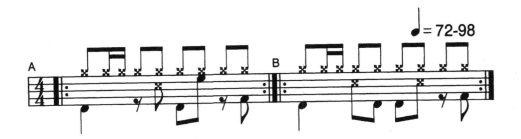

MEASURE A

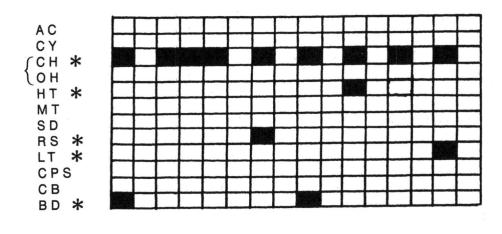

MEASURE B

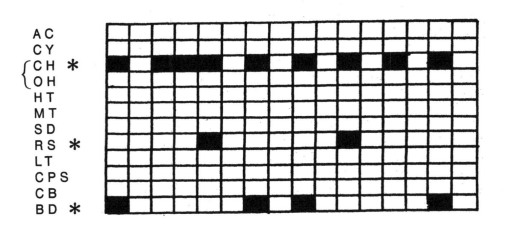

BREAK

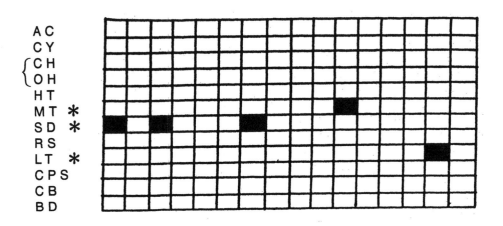

Blues 1

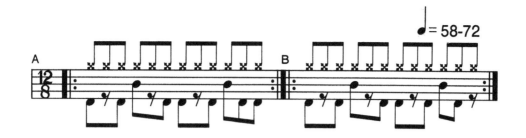

MEASURE A

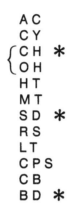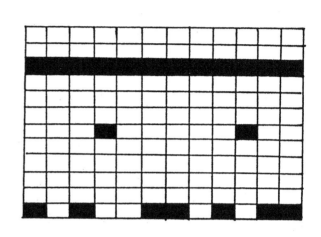

MEASURE B

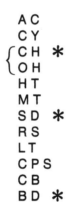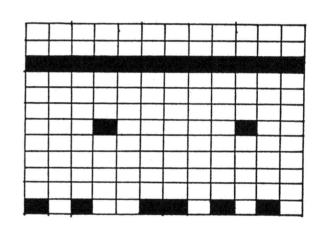

BREAK

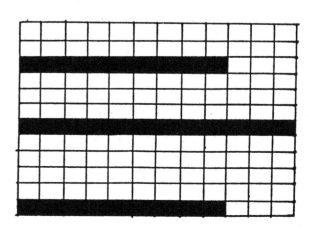

57

Blues 2

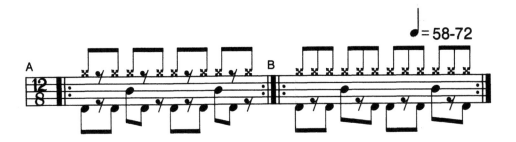

MEASURE A

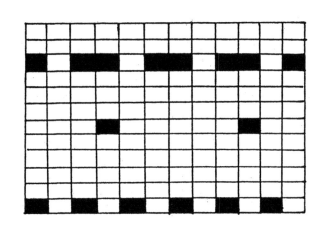

MEASURE B

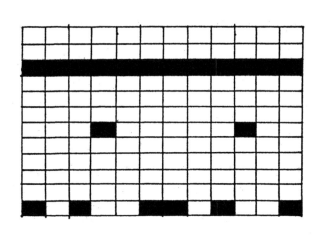

BREAK

Swing 1

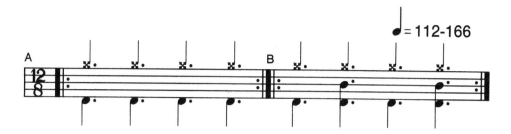

MEASURE A

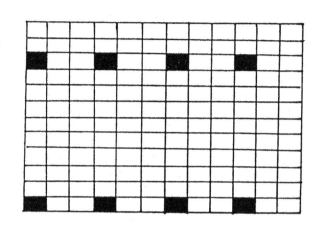

MEASURE B

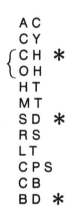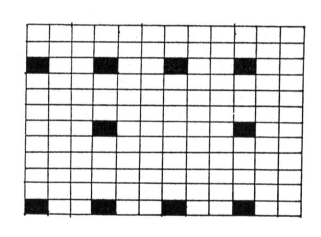

BREAK

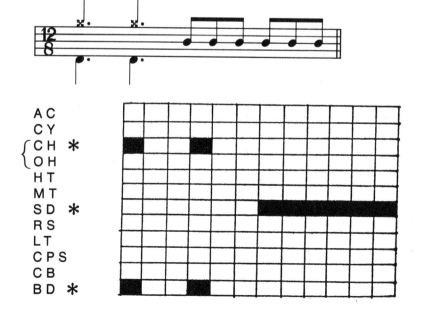

59

Swing 2

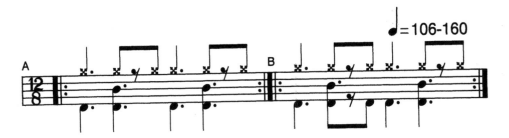

MEASURE A

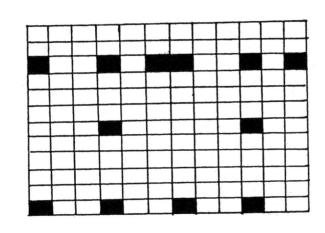

MEASURE B

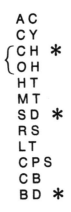
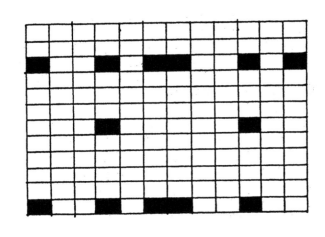

BREAK

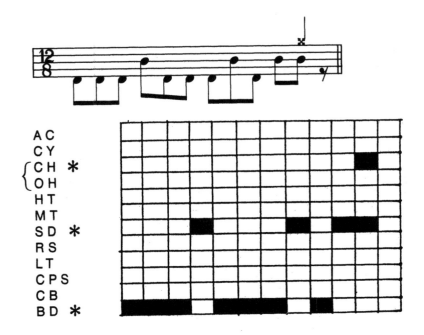

Swing 3

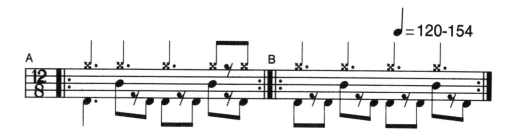

MEASURE A

 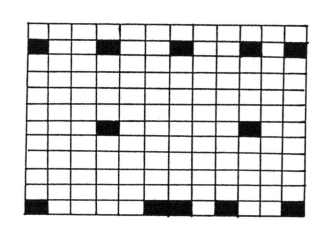

MEASURE B

 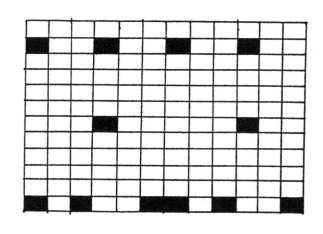

BREAK

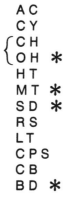 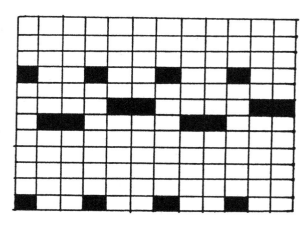

Shuffle 1

MEASURE A

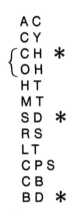
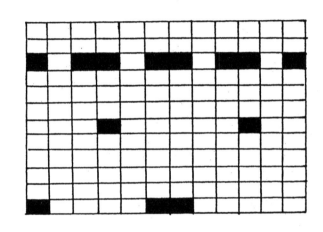

MEASURE B

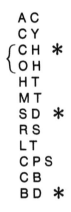
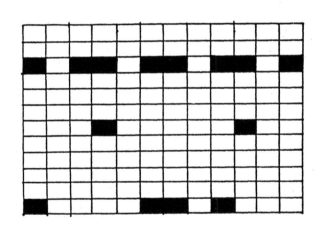

BREAK

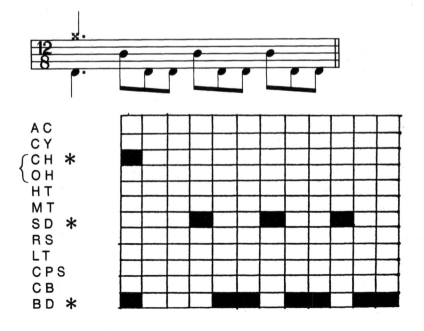

Shuffle 2

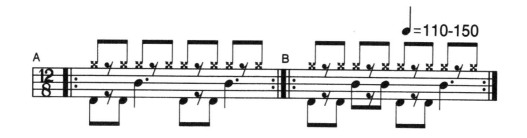

MEASURE A

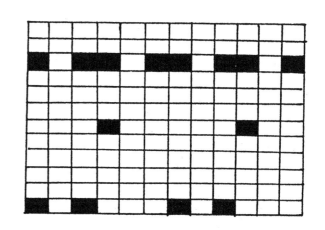

MEASURE B

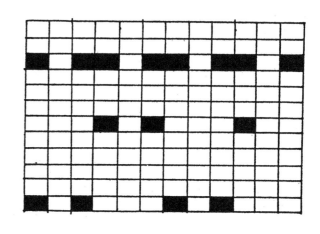

BREAK

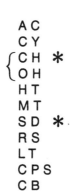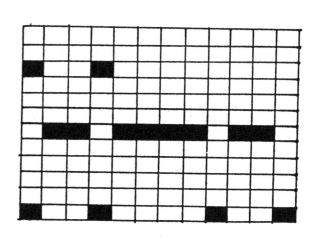

Samba 1

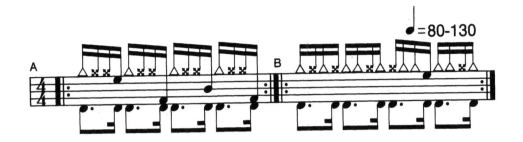

MEASURE A

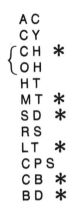
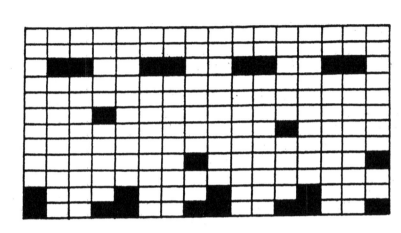

AC
CY
CH *
OH
HT
MT *
SD *
RS
LT *
CPS
CB *
BD *

MEASURE B

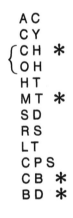
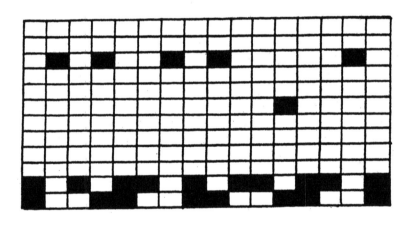

AC
CY
CH *
OH
HT
MT *
SD
RS
LT
CPS
CB *
BD *

BREAK

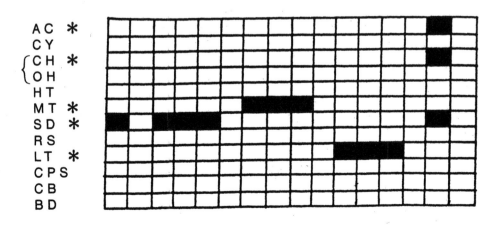

AC *
CY
CH *
OH
HT
MT *
SD *
RS
LT *
CPS
CB
BD

64

Samba 2

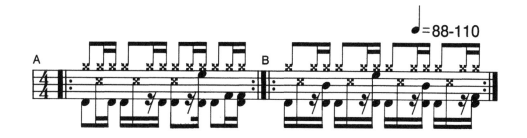

MEASURE A

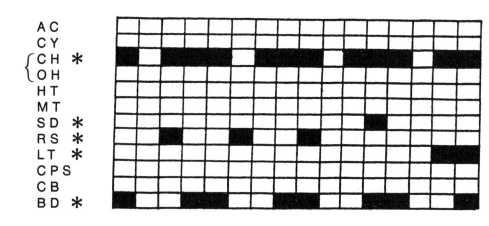

MEASURE B

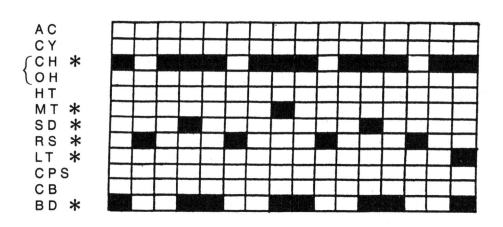

BREAK

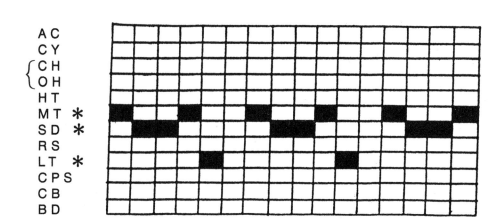

Samba 3

MEASURE A

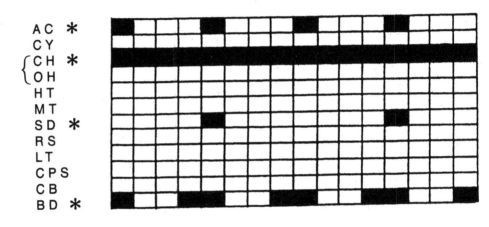

MEASURE B

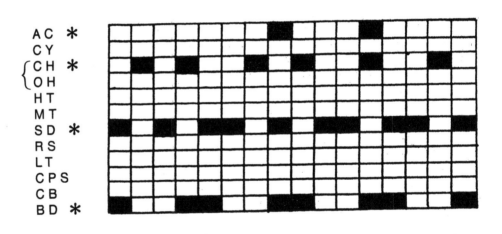

BREAK

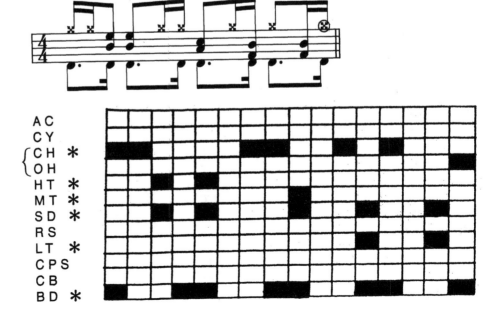

Bossa Nova 1

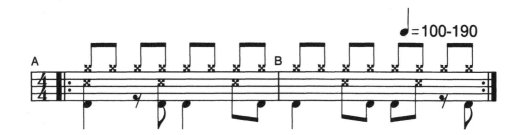

MEASURE A

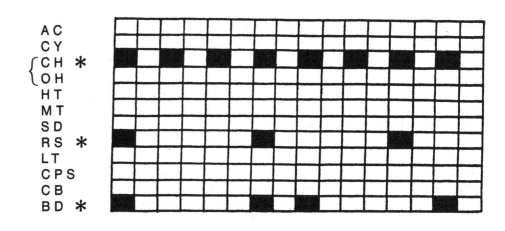

MEASURE B

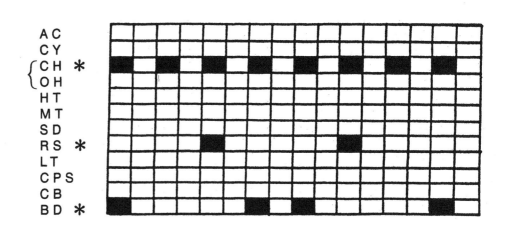

BREAK

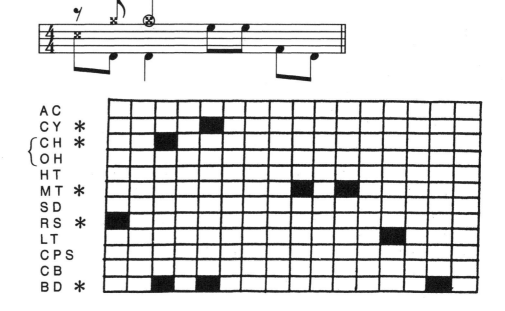

67

Bossa Nova 2

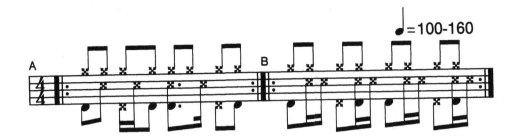

MEASURE A

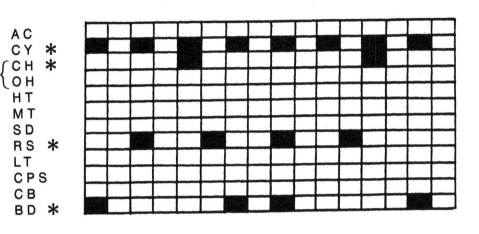

MEASURE B

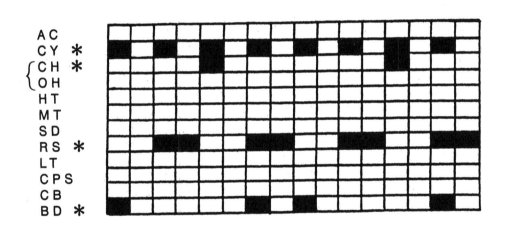

BREAK

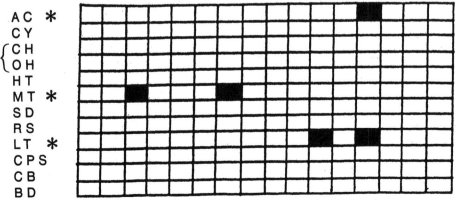

Cha-Cha

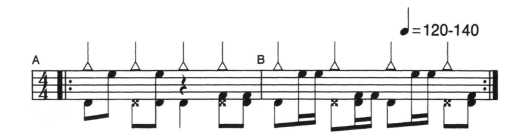

MEASURE A

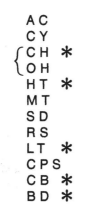 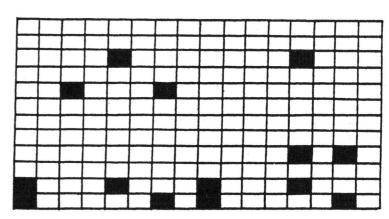

MEASURE B

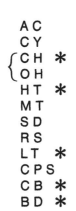 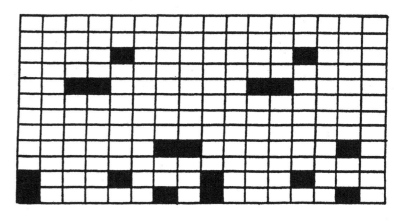

BREAK

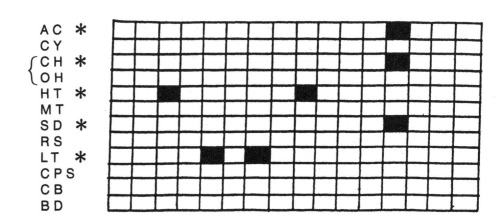

Twist 1

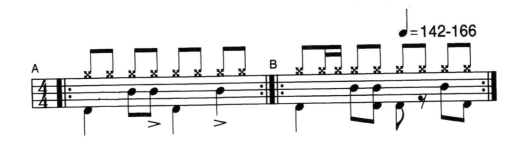

MEASURE A

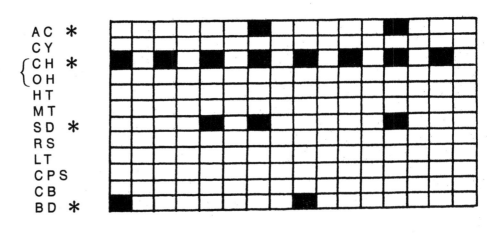

MEASURE B

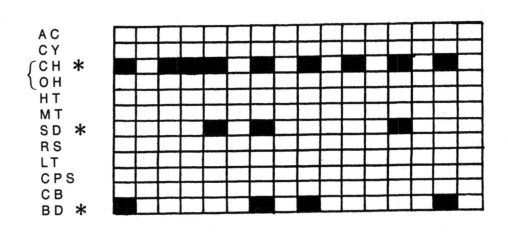

BREAK

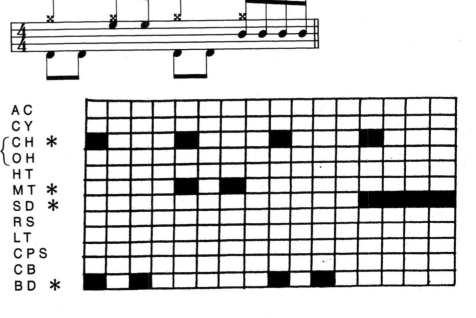

Twist 2

MEASURE A

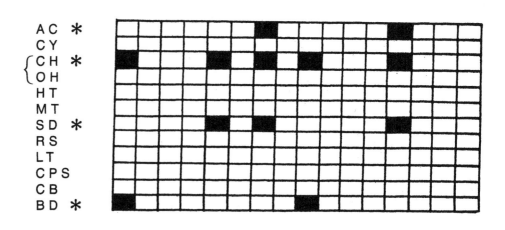

MEASURE B

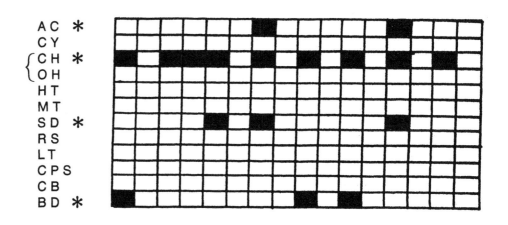

BREAK

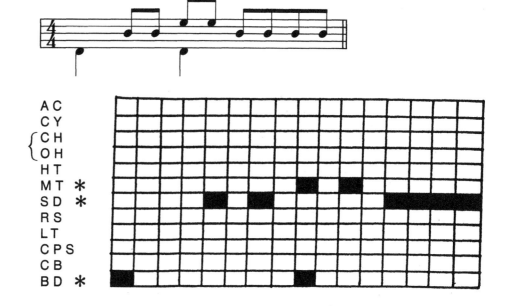

71

Ska

MEASURE A

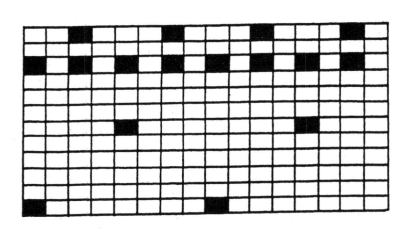

MEASURE B

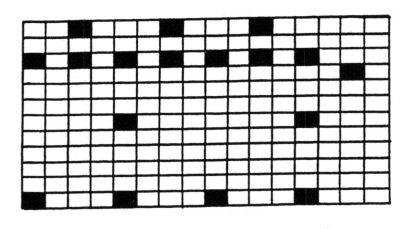

BREAK

Endings

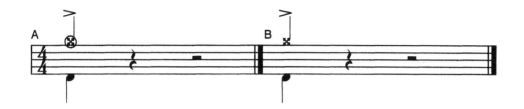

MEASURE A

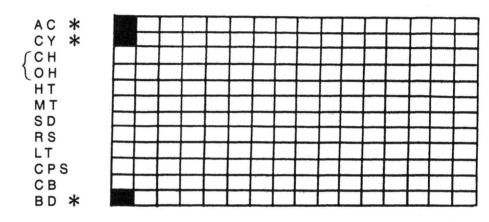

MEASURE B

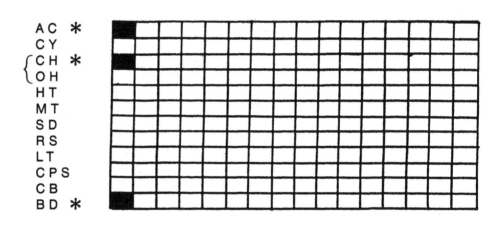

Original Patterns

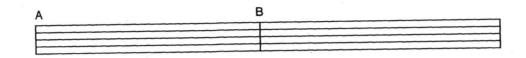

MEASURE A

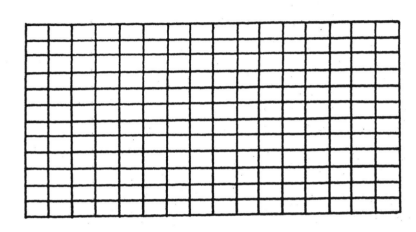

MEASURE B

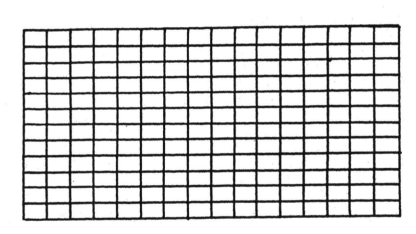

BREAK

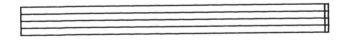

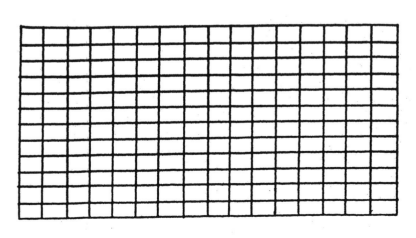

Original Patterns

MEASURE A

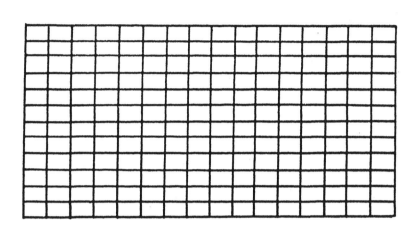

MEASURE B

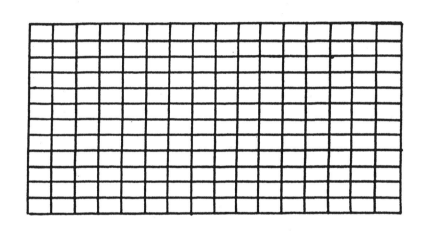

BREAK

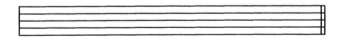

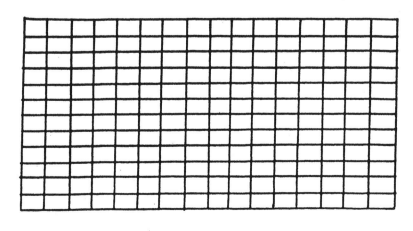

Original Patterns

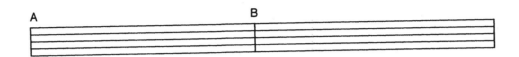

MEASURE A

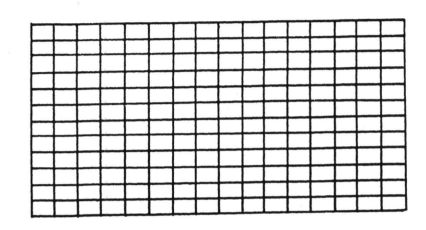

MEASURE B

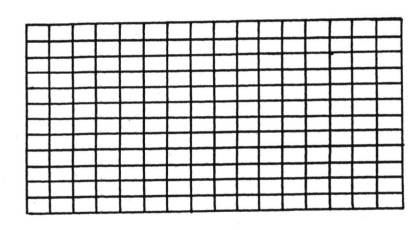

BREAK

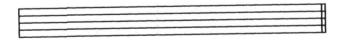

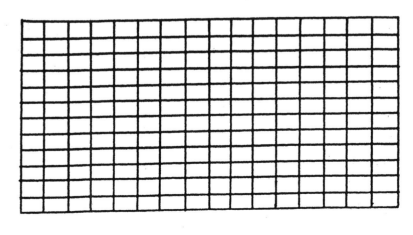

Original Patterns

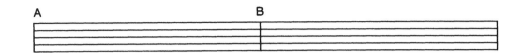

MEASURE A

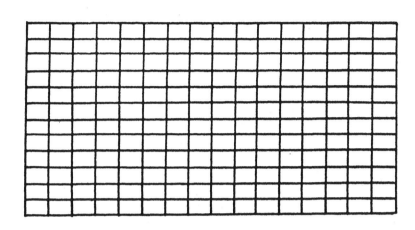

MEASURE B

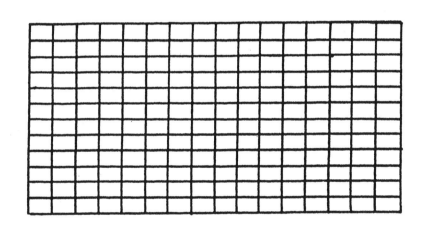

BREAK

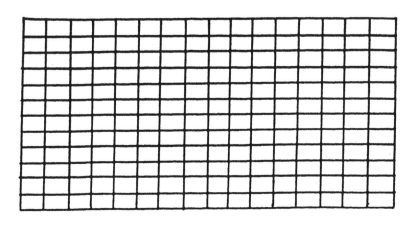

Original Patterns

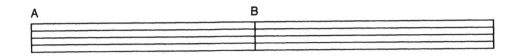

MEASURE A

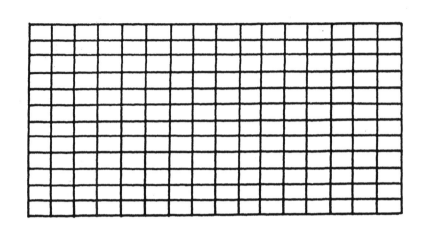

MEASURE B

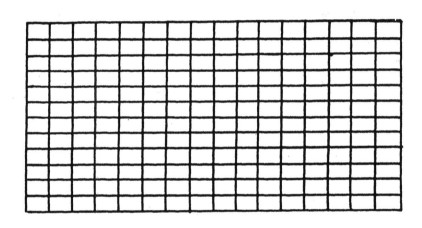

BREAK

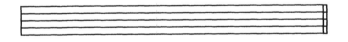

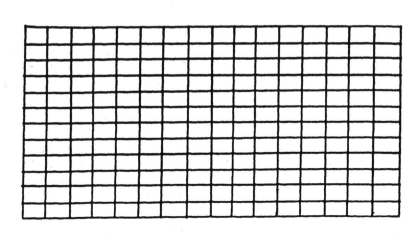

Original Patterns

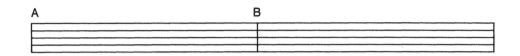

MEASURE A

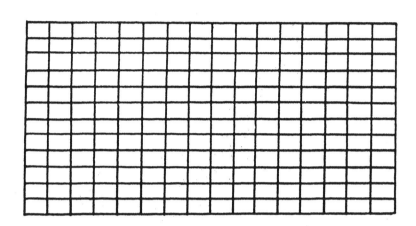

MEASURE B

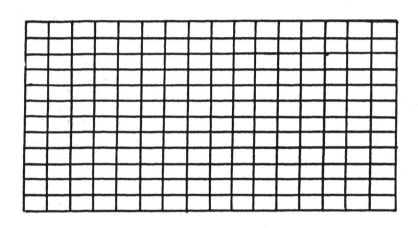

BREAK

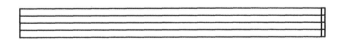

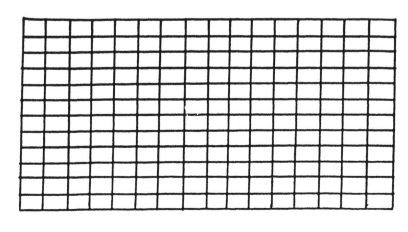